TEARS OF PAIN:
My Life with Autism

Marc Rivera

"TEARS OF PAIN: My Life with Autism," by Marc Rivera. ISBN 978-1-62137-253-0.

Published 2013 by Virtualbookworm.com Publishing Inc., P.O. Box 9949, College Station, TX 77842, US. ©2013, Marc Rivera. All rights reserved. No part of this publication may be reproduced, stored in a retrieval system, or transmitted in any form or by any means, electronic, mechanical, recording or otherwise, without the prior written permission of Marc Rivera.

Manufactured in the United States of America.

To all my fellow A- Listers and their families who are still struggling to be understood

I have tried to recreate events, and conversations from my memories of them. Some names, identifying details and places have been changed to protect the privacy of individuals.

I wish to thank the following professionals for their contributions, knowledge and other help in creating this book:

Susan M. Shuman, Editor
Marilee Emerson, M.Ed.
Barbara Upshaw-Mayers, Graphic Designer

Table of Contents

Foreword
Chapter One
    Welcome to my World 1
Chapter Two
    Doing Time in Kindergarten 3
Chapter Three
    Elementary School: A Nightmare 5
Chapter Four
    On the Road with Angst 12
Chapter Five
    A Fourth Grader's Angst 17
Chapter Six
    Jive in Grade Five 23
Chapter Seven
    Home, Sweet Home 25
Chapter Eight
    Home School 28
Chapter Nine
    High School: Instant Replay 30
Chapter Ten
    Ms. Quintana: Teacher Dearest 33
Chapter Eleven
    Misadventures with my Classmates 39
Chapter Twelve
    Making Friends 101: Waving 45
Chapter Thirteen
    Marc vs. Vocational School 49

Chapter Fourteen
    My First Job...51
Chapter Fifteen
    About Me and My Life 55

Foreword

FROM TIME TO TIME, we are privileged with person-first accounts of individuals with disabilities. It takes both physical and emotional effort to share such personal accounts. Courage, too.

For this reason, I believe it is <u>critical</u> that we read, we listen to, and we learn from these first-person accounts.

Marc Rivera is an "Asperger A-lister," a term Marc's editor coined to describe him and others with autism spectrum disorders.

One of Marc's unique talents is his steel-trap memory, which can be both a blessing and a curse. Remembering every experience (like it just happened) can quickly become a burden, especially when your negative experiences outweigh your positive ones.

While being on an A-list may sound cool, it has its disadvantages. Marc's private journal-turned-book captures a snapshot for teachers, parents, students – all of us – that describe the quiet suffering of a young man who is different.

Dr. Temple Grandin, a well-known A-lister, author, and autism advocate was quoted with this observation about her own differences: "Different, not less."

Marc's desire through his school years can be summed up to these simple actions: to be understood, and treated with fairness and respect.

Marc's account of his experiences of being misunderstood, criticized, and living in a state of perpetual anxiety are opportunities for us all to consider (or re-consider) our own interactions with individuals who are different from us.

How would you be portrayed in another person's memoir?

How would an individual who remembers everything remember your actions?

These are two profound questions to consider; for some they may even be a revelation.

I often say, if you haven't met someone with autism, chances are you will. Last year, prevalence rates for autism spectrum disorders was 1 in 88. That means statistically, it's in our best interest to know a little something about the people who come into our lives, as students, classmates, neighbors and friends.

When Marc and I spoke about his experiences, he agreed when I suggested that every A-lister has shed tears of pain.
What if, by our own interactions with others, we had a chance to reduce the number of tears?

"Kindness matters." Marc says this in his book. It's a statement of fact and an observation.

For Marc, it is a prayer.

While *Tears of Pain* offers teachers, parents and students a learning opportunity, it offers Marc so much more.

Writing this book was a healing journey. It's an invitation to look into the heart of a young man who has struggled to find his place in the world.

As a special educator for 25 years, I recognize the value of first-person accounts. There are still lessons to be learned, voices to be heard, and future hurts to avoid.

Learning to listen may indeed be one of the most important skills we can develop to live in an ever changing, ever diverse world.

Kindness matters.

Marilee Emerson, M.Ed.
Special Educator, Person-Centered Planner
Founder MyMarilee.com
Orlando, Florida

Chapter One

Welcome to my World

HI! YOU KNOW ME: I'm that one kid in class who is well, kind of different. I'm smart in a lot of ways, good at math and science. I don't care for sports or fashion, and I don't fit-in anywhere. I'm the kid you like to call a nerd, geek, weirdo and Lord knows what else. In school, I'm usually the one getting pushed around, teased and bullied for being different. I think a lot of you do that because you are afraid of people and things that are different from you. I don't fit your idea of normal so, therefore, I must be punished. Is that it? Because I sometimes make inappropriate responses, seem naïve or immature, and don't "get" jokes or understand the implications of facial expressions—means I am lesser-than, to you, right?

Wrong! I have a condition called Asperger's Syndrome, which is a form of autism. Take note that I said I *have* Asperger's, *it* doesn't have *me*. It's not contagious so you don't have to be afraid of catching it from saying hello to me, or even including me in conversations. My brain is wired differently than yours, that's all it is.

Here is something else you don't know: there are some famous and successful people who have been diagnosed with Asperger's. People like Satoshi Tajiri, the guy who invented Pokémon™, Vernon L. Smith, Nobel Laureate in Economics, and Phillipa "Pip" Brown (aka *Ladyhawke*), the indie rock star, were all diagnosed with the very same condition *I* have. I'll bet you wouldn't gang up on those people because they are different, would you?

There are some plusses to being on the Asperger's A-list, by the way. My memory is phenomenal. I am creative, have unique interests, and can easily catch and retain the smallest details. I'd make a great friend too, since people with Asperger's tend to be loyal, dependable, and honest. On the other hand, there are some obvious disadvantages to this condition. It's hard for me to discern a lie, I avoid eye contact and don't like hugging. Loud noises freak me out and I have trouble recognizing people's voice tones and interpreting body language.

There's no doubt about it. You and I live in two different worlds, but that doesn't mean we can't learn from one another and be friends.

The following pages will describe what life is like on the Asperger's A-List. My hope is to help you better understand what it's like to be me.

You are welcome in my world. Please, don't be afraid to let me inside yours.

Chapter Two

Doing Time in Kindergarten

MY FIRST REAL INTERACTION with the outside world was when my parents sent me to a New York day care center. I cried nearly every day—separation anxiety. I wanted to be home with my grandmother, who took care of me while my parents worked. I became incontinent and refused to eat. Many times, they sent me home at noon, which was fine with me!

One of the teachers, a man, had a loud, booming voice which frightened me terribly. Most kids with Asperger's can't stand loud noises of any kind. Just my luck, I ended up in his room. That's when things really went haywire! Out of fear, I cried constantly. Nobody understood why, nor did anyone try to find out. I guess they just wrote me off as a crybaby problem child.

They used to do show and tell at the day care center. One of the kids was doing his show and tell. It was a tiny little toy bus and the kid let me play with it. Immediately, it was like if I had formed an instant attachment to it. The people were trying to get me to give the bus back to the boy and I wouldn't give it back. I don't remember if I was crying or not, but I got used to the bus that I wouldn't give it back. Eventually, I gave the bus back to the boy but it was quite an ordeal. I wasn't used to this, I didn't have to deal with anything like that at home.

I didn't like it there at the day care center.

Chapter Three

Elementary School: A Nightmare

GEE, AND I THOUGHT kindergarten was tough! From the first day I was a marked man—an outcast. It all started over my not being able to eat all of the food on my plate when the cafeteria ladies brought it to us. Sometimes, like everyone, I am just not hungry. Other times, again, like everyone else, I didn't care for the type of food. One time, the teacher tried to make me eat an egg sandwich in which I had absolutely no interest. She actually started to scream at me when I explained that I didn't like it. When that didn't work, she spoke to me in a stern, angry voice. I will never forget that tone of voice.

"Get up!" Her voice was lethal and low. My bladder felt weak. I was so frightened and confused that I began to cry. Unable to stop the steady flow of tears, they sent me home early. A similar situation occurred over glass of milk that I didn't want to drink. It seemed as though every morning this teacher screamed at me about something. Eventually, I figured out a solution—just tell the teachers that I had already eaten breakfast at home. I was hungry, but at least no one yelled at me and made me nervous.

With that problem solved another challenge presented itself: my peers. They were just plain mean. This one kid named Donald always wanted to play rough. He knew I didn't like it because I told him so. He didn't care. He just kept hitting me—and this is the part I *really* didn't "get" — Donald would ask, "Who hit you?" Then he'd hit me again, and repeat, "Who hit you, huh? Who hit you?" Clearly, he was the one hitting me, so it made no sense as to why he would ask such a question. Bewildered, I just stood there while he hit me trying to figure out what I was missing. The situation left me feeling confused, scared and anxious. I don't remember if I cried or not. If I didn't, I sure wanted to!

There was also a Spanish kid named Norberto who liked to put his hands on my face. I hated when he did that and he knew it. When he got tired of touching my face, Norberto would aggravate me by repeatedly asking, "What's this?" "What's this?" No matter how many times I would tell him what *that* was he'd keep on asking. It made no sense to me why someone would do that. Confused and anxious, I would burst into tears and Norberto would laugh and call me a crybaby.

I couldn't catch a break!

Oh, and then there was the fateful day when the other kids figured out that by screaming my name like a pack of wolves would make me cry—angry tears of pain. Asperger A-list people cannot tolerate loud noises, so you can imagine what a gang of screaming kids did to my mind. I didn't understand why they did that. I was right there and could hear them. They didn't have to scream.

This was one of the many times that I wished I had a friend.

That's what it's like for some of us with Asperger's Syndrome. We simply don't view the world in the same way you do. We see it all through a slightly distorted lens. It follows, then, that we would process what we see and experience in a distorted manner. In addition, it is difficult for us to assess a situation accurately, gauge people's moods and intentions, and discern what is and is not, acceptable behavior. In other words, half the time we don't even realize we are being bullied. Rather than fight back or stick up for ourselves, we apply logic and critical thinking in an attempt to draw a rational conclusion. While we try to make sense of a senseless situation, we're being teased, tormented and even beat up. This is what triggers the anxiety attacks. Asperger kids are an easy mark. It's like walking around with a "please, kick me," sign on our backs and most of you are all too willing to do just that.

Speaking of anxiety, I can still hear my grandmother yelling, "Come back here!"

After school, the bus would drop me off right in front of my house. Every day, my grandmother would wait for me at the front door. It was a Friday afternoon — I'll never forget it. After the bus dropped me off, I saw my grandmother waiting at the front door and rather than going inside the house, I ran away. To this day, I don't know why but I just began running like a wild man. My grandmother tried to chase me, yelling, "Marc, come back!" I just kept running.

I ran and ran with no place to go.

There was a barking dog in front of one of the houses I had passed, which made me run even faster. I am terrified of dogs. Eventually, I ended up at my Aunt Maria's house which was a few blocks away from my house. I knocked, but Auntie didn't answer the door. She didn't live there anymore.

With nowhere else to go, I began walking back to my house. That's when I saw my mom. She was running up the street, frantically calling my name. We ran to each other, and she put her arms in a big, perfect hug. There's nothing like a hug from your mom, you know?

More than anything in the world, I needed that hug.

When we finished hugging, together, my mom and I walked home. During my absence, someone had called the police. The policewoman asked me if the dog scared me and I said no. I don't know why I ran away from my house. It was as if I was in my own world or something. My mom and grandmother got worried. They were scared I would be hurt. I was scared, too. Looking back, all kinds of bad things could have happened to me.

Not only were many of the kids bullies, a few of my teachers were, too! I thought the teachers were there to look out for kids and help them learn, but apparently not. They could be every bit as cruel. I wonder why teachers had no clue when it came to kids with Asperger's Disorder. Didn't they learn that kids like me process information differently? You would think there would be a class on Asperger's and autism, or something.

While still in New York, I transferred to another school for third grade. It was great because it was close enough to home that my mom was able to walk me to and from school every day. It gave me such joy not to ride that school bus.

Unfortunately, my joy was short-lived. The new school turned out to be just another nightmare.

In the new school, I was "mainstreamed," meaning that I went from being in a class with a few students, to a class of over twenty students. My teacher was beyond frustrating. Her name was Ms. Gordon. Being in her class was dreadful—what I experienced with her, I wouldn't wish on anyone. You can imagine my relief when my family decided to move to Florida later that year.

Ms. Gordon constantly yelled, "Marc, you're not listening!" and frequently wrote on my homework pages "This is not the homework!" Ms. Gordon used a harsh tone of voice with me, which made me exceedingly nervous. She would also write down "Did he do this by himself?" on my assignments. If she only knew how hard I was trying to adjust to this new "mainstream" situation! She had no clue, but she *did* have a mean streak.

One time she made me cry when she snapped, "When I ask if you have anything for me, it means you should give me your lunch money at the beginning of the day!"

Okay, well, why didn't she say that then? How was I to know *that's* what she meant? She was talking to me as if she didn't understand why *I* didn't understand. I felt so lost. My inherent shyness didn't help matters, either. At school, I lived in a world of perpetual anxiety. I was even afraid to open my notebook for fear that Ms. Gordon would yell at me for whatever I did or didn't do. That, coupled with dealing with my bullying peers was enough to push anyone over the edge.

My confusion in school escalated, as I was no longer in special education classes. My parents were aware of the situation and tried to transfer me to another teacher but the school would not cooperate. My mom constantly visited the school to speak with the principal. I tried so hard to understand what was going on, but no matter what I did, this teacher was never happy. She refused to cut me *any* slack, and made my life a living hell. No kid should have to experience a living hell. I felt alone, afraid and completely lost. It seemed as if I was a stranger from another planet. To me, it seemed that Ms. Gordon neither cared nor understood that I was struggling to adapt to the change. My world became more frightening and confusing by the day. I was worried all the time. It's a wonder I didn't snap. The very thought of going to school triggered angry tears of pain. I hated that place.

Oh, how I *hated* that place!

Chapter Four

On the Road with Angst

I HAD BECOME ACCUSTOMED to the little bus that came to pick me up for school each day. It was safe and I could deal with it. Then, when I changed schools, my mom would walk me there and back, which was great. No bullies—no problems.

Then we moved to Florida.

This move brought about many changes.

Asperger kids are not fond of change. In fact, we are terrified of it.

First, my dad's job was such that he left for work at around 5:00am. My mother worked early hours as well, and my brother was already at school by the time my classes began.

Things were looking grim.

There was no choice but to ride the bus, the big bus that carried bullies. The terror started the moment I would board and continued throughout the day. Try to imagine what it's like to wake up every morning with fear and dread. Then have the day play out just as you imagined, sometimes worse. If it wasn't the mean kids teasing me until I would cry tears of pain, it was the teachers yelling at me because they didn't understand Asperger's Syndrome. Then, it was back on the bus for some more bad-natured taunting. In the afternoons and evenings, I would struggle with homework, but who can concentrate when there is the next days' bullying to worry about?

Can you imagine being afraid of going to school? Anything could happen there, and it was never good. I never knew when or how the bullying would begin, what the theme would be — bullies are innovative — or the outcome. Let alone whether I'd end up being physically injured. Inner pain, hurt feelings and humiliation were a given.

The only word that accurately describes my school years is **torture**.

One day, I could no longer take it. The bus stop was a short distance from our apartment and as I walked, I hesitated. I was taking my sweet time. I stopped here and there, as if I had all the time in the world and no particular place to go.

This lady, who apparently lived in the same apartment complex, came up to me and asked if I was aware that the bus had left without me. I failed to respond. She then proceeded to escort me back home. My grandmother greeted us at the door and she and the lady spoke in Spanish. I am not sure exactly what they said, but when my dad got home, he too became aware that the bus left without me.

Then my whole family knew. My dad's tone of voice scared me. He usually didn't talk to me that way and it was unsettling and confusing. My mom seemed angry, too. Neither of them understood why I missed the bus. When it happened again the next day, and the day after that, my whole family was mad at me. They didn't understand that the reason I purposely missed the bus was because I did not want to go to school. I mean, I *really* did not want to be there.

For a few days after that, my mom walked me to the bus stop to make sure I would get to school.

On the bus were kids ranging in age from kindergarten to the fifth-grade. Nobody wanted to sit with me. It was hard to find a place to sit but the bus driver couldn't move the bus unless everyone was seated. This always made me nervous because I never knew where to sit. No matter where I sat, it would bother someone. I was afraid that if I accidentally bothered someone, they might start taunting and teasing me. My mere existence seemed to set them off — the bullies, I mean. What was I supposed to do? What is it these kids wanted from me?

I especially hated riding the bus because the mean kids would ask me if I liked "doogies." I didn't know what a "doogie" was so I said I liked them. I learned to always say that I liked everything since saying I didn't like something would make some kids angry, no matter what it was. So, I said I liked "doogies" which made everyone laugh. The noise was unbearable, I felt confused. I mean, what *was* a "doogie?" Why was it funny to like them? Was it wrong not to like them? I didn't dare ask.

One of the worst things that ever happened on the bus was when Anita asked me if I loved this girl named Bela, whom I didn't even know. Since I always said yes to everything, I said yes, I loved Bela, whoever she was. Well, Bela acted as if it was one of the biggest insults of the century to have someone like me love her. She was actually *offended*! I was the one who was offended, not to mention embarrassed, tense and bewildered. Of course, *my* feelings never came in to question. That's how it is when bullies are involved.

I hated riding that bus. Hated it!

The situation escalated when they started asking me if I liked boys and other questions that I am not going to mention. *That's* when I started saying "No." They still asked those questions to try to get me to say yes. Over, and over, and over . . . they would ask the same stupid questions. Don't ask me why. I don't know.

Another thing that puzzled me at school was that kids were always asking me to give them my loose-leaf notebook paper. They would ask for six or seven pages at a time, everyday! I often wonder what my parents must have thought— always having to buy more paper for me. What I didn't understand was why the kids asked me for my paper when they had plenty of their own. I always gave it to them though, no telling what might have happened otherwise. I was afraid to find out, but I felt as if they were taking advantage of me.

Chapter Five

A Fourth Grader's Angst

DURING THE SUMMER BETWEEN third and fourth grade my family moved into a new house. This meant I would begin the fourth grade in a new school. My teacher's name was Ms. Enfield. I had no end of problems that year.

It seemed that I was never in my seat during class. I felt lost and everything seemed like it was on fast-forward. Things happened so fast I couldn't keep up with the changes, and all that was going on. My grades had gone downhill, probably because I didn't do my homework. For some reason, I just didn't bother to bring it home with me after school. One time though, I did bring it home and my mom helped me with it so I knew it was right. In fact, I was actually *looking forward* to handing in my paper so Ms. Enfield would be proud of how well I had done.

Regrettably, I threw my homework away, instead. I don't know why. Sometimes kids with Asperger's do things like that. Stuff just . . . happens. If I could explain why, I would.

What really made my head spin was when there were essay questions on tests. The answers, of course, had to be coherent and well thought out. Mine were neither. When I started to write, my brain would throw a bunch of information at me all at once. I didn't understand what my brain was telling me and it wouldn't slow down. I did the best I could with a hurricane of information banging around in my head.

As far as bullies, there were just as many at this new school as there were at my old one. PE class was a horrific ordeal. No one ever wanted me on his or her team. The boys would argue over whose team would be stuck with me. The humiliation and pain brought a flood of hot, stinging tears. To make matters worse, I was a one-man comedy show, a source of laughter and amusement to my classmates. For example, the fact that I could not manage sit-ups no matter how hard I tried had my "peers" in stitches. Then there was the time I was unable to get my double-knotted gym shoes back on my feet. Double knots are difficult for me to manage. My fingers refused to cooperate with my brain, and vice versa. The kids laughed loudly as I nervously fumbled with the laces. I began to cry out of sheer panic and fear. The noise of their laughter didn't help matters either. I finally told them that I didn't know how to tie my shoes, which was a white lie just to get them away from me. I knew how to tie my shoes, it's just that I couldn't manage it right at that moment. That only made them laugh louder. There was no way to win.

For some reason they liked pulling my pants down, too. They said, "It's the style now, Marc!" I didn't care if it was the style or not. My underwear shouldn't be showing and that's the end of it. Nobody's underwear should be showing.

That's why they call it *under*wear!

I would pull my pants back up but the boys just yanked them down again. It hurt my feelings bad. None of that made any sense to me. All they wanted to do was make fun of me and take advantage. Looking back, I wish I had told my parents about all the trouble I had in school. Maybe they could have done something to help and protect me.

Art class wasn't much better. One morning I tried to sit with Davy and Carl, but they made it clear that I was not welcome. We went back and forth for a few minutes, I tried to talk them into letting me sit down, but it was useless. They physically pushed me away. Finally, my feelings were so badly hurt that I was unable to choke back the tears. In addition, I was scared. Why was the world so mean? I had tried so hard! What had I done to deserve to be treated this way? It was puzzling.

I went to the front office and stayed there the rest of the day, refusing to return to Ms. Enfield's class. All I wanted to do was go home.

Whenever I was at school, all I wanted was to be at home.

The next day I pretended to be sick and my mom let me stay home. I was able to enjoy a full day with neither bullies nor teasing. It was a good day. The following day I pretended to be sick again, but my mom didn't believe me.

"Marc, you are going to school!"

My heart sank. I felt nervous inside and wanted to vomit. Slowly, I got myself ready for school. Eventually I left the house and went to the bus stop, then turned around and walked right back home. My grandmother began yelling at me in Spanish. I'm not sure of her exact words, but I assume she was telling me to go back to the bus stop.

As I was walking, the bus met me half way. I just stood there and looked at it. The driver opened the door and waited for me to board, but I couldn't (or wouldn't) get on that bus. I just stood there, staring. My feet refused to move. Finally, the driver shrugged and left without me. I watched it drive away and went back into the house. It was then that I called 911 and told them that I was unable to breathe. I was having a panic attack.

Boy, did I get in trouble that day! My dad and brother scared me with their voices. I knew it would happen but it scared me all the same. Even my mom made me a little nervous that day. In spite of the way things turned out, it was better than being on that bus. I guess the lesson we all learned was that I was prone to panic attacks.

From then on, my dad began driving me to and from school. It's much better to be picked-up than picked-on. I worried so much about what may happen to me on the bus, coupled with the fact that none of the boys would let me sit with them. This is what caused my fear of school busses and going to school. With my dad I felt safe, finally, at least until I arrived at school.

Did I tell you about what it was like during lunchtime at the cafeteria? What a screamer. You may have guessed that I was not welcome to sit with the other kids during lunch since they didn't want me around any other time. In fact, a few times I ended up standing as I ate my lunch. I'm not a horse! I'm a human being who is supposed to sit down for meals.

Have *you* ever eaten *your* lunch standing up?

One time I was standing in line waiting to get my tray and one of the kids, Cameron, accused me of butting in line. He pushed me into a bunch of other kids, and they pushed me back to Cameron. This back and forth business went on for a while—I don't know how long. I remember getting scared because they were laughing and began pushing me harder and faster. I was getting dizzy and felt like throwing up. Somehow, it came to a stop. I don't remember how, though.

Later in class, Cameron slammed his desk into mine and smashed my finger. I don't know why he did that. Wasn't pushing me back and forth in the lunch line enough? Then, when Ms. Enfield got mad and used that tone of voice that scares me, Cameron blamed *me* when *he* was the one that smashed *his* desk into mine! Everything was happening fast again and I couldn't keep up with it. Tears of pain stung my eyes and I couldn't stop them from surging down my cheeks. Ms. Enfield told me to stop crying. She didn't understand at all. She went to get a Band-Aid™ from her desk but I didn't need one. My finger hurt but it wasn't cut. Besides, my pain was on the inside, but nobody knew because I couldn't tell them. I was panicking and confused.

It was just another bewildering day in the life of Marc Rivera.

Chapter Six

Jive in Grade Five

THEN I BEGAN THE fifth grade. The best words to describe that year are **bad news**. I had even more problems than I did in the fourth grade; and I cried more if you could imagine that. One stellar memory was of an episode in PE class. I was supposed to be on Rob's team, but of course, Rob didn't want me. The teacher made Rob accept me as a member of his team, but Rob certainly wasn't welcoming. He growled at me. Can you imagine? Rob actually growled! I was beyond terrified and began to cry. I mean, seriously, why would a kid growl like an animal just because I was on his team? It was a game—a stupid PE class—not Desert Storm! It made no sense to me as I tried to puzzle it out in my mind. The bullying continued in the new school.

Another time, these two boys in my PE class, Kris and Jared, wanted me to dance for them. I didn't want to but they kept telling me to dance so I finally did. I danced a couple of times, but then I refused to dance anymore. I didn't want to dance! More than that, I knew they were taking advantage of me. Even one of the girls, Teri, kept asking me to dance over, and over, but I wouldn't. They didn't understand why I wouldn't dance anymore, and I certainly didn't understand why they wanted me to dance.

There was another boy named Byron who wanted me to trade seats with him in class. He said if I didn't trade with him, he would cut my head off. He then said that he wasn't kidding. Those words cut me deeper than any knife ever could. I cried hard tears of pain over that.

Hurt feelings are something that stays with you. A punch in the nose will heal, but pain inside remains forever.

The rest of my fifth year in school continued in much the same fashion. Kris pushing and shoving me around, Teri and Byron calling me an idiot and dodo bird, and teasing me about my hair and saying I smelled bad. Those were just a few of the humiliating things I endured.

You know, the term "idiot" is one of the ugliest words you can fling at someone. If you look it up in the dictionary, it talks about an idiot being one of the lowest forms of mental retardation. It's better to be labeled "stupid," than to be called an "idiot." People don't realize how much words can hurt someone. On the other hand, maybe they do. Maybe belittling someone else makes certain people feel better about themselves. Like, in order for them to feel superior, they have to make someone else feel inferior.

Chapter Seven

Home, Sweet Home

LIFE AT HOME PRESENTED its challenges too, but nothing like the torment I dealt with at school. Sometimes I'd watch the *Ren & Stimpy* cartoon in which the song *Claire de Lune* was played. The song has a sad, haunting melody that always made me cry. It made *Stimpy* cry too. My mom asked me once why I was crying and I told her it was because *Stimpy* had no friends and was an outcast like me. It really reminded me of the bad things that had happened in school, and the other bad things that I knew were going to happen there. My mom told me not to watch the show if it was going to make me cry and she did not want to see me sad. It hurt my mom a lot when I was unhappy or crying.

My brother, Michael and I are closer now than we used to be. When I was much younger, he used to get mad at me a lot, and use that certain tone of voice that scared me. For example, when I was about seven-years-old I destroyed a book called "The Official Nintendo Players' Guide." This mistake occurred on April 10, 1989. One of the plusses of having Asperger's is that I am good at remembering dates and times. Anyway, Michael, who was fourteen at the time, used that tone of voice when he asked why I broke the book. I'm apt to say that he was yelling at me. Then, I showed my mom and she yelled at me too. It wasn't a good day for me.

Another time, about three years later, I annoyed Michael while his friends were visiting. I started talking about a T.V. show I liked called *Where in the World is Carmen Sandiego?* and acting silly. Michael was embarrassed, and told me to stop acting stupid. I began to cry and Michael asked why I was faking the tears. After his friends left, Michael asked me to start acting like a ten-year old rather than a four-year old. I didn't understand what he meant.

One time in November 1990, I said that I was not feeling well. I pretended to not feel well because I did not want to go to school. I was having problems at school that time. I pretended that I could not walk properly. My brother saw me walking and he said that I could walk. I pretended not to walk properly because I did not want to go to school.

My brother has done some very nice things for me, and taught me a lot over the years. One of the most useful skills he taught me how to take telephone messages. It was 1994 and I had a hard time answering the telephone. When my grandmother and I were home alone, I had to answer the phone because she didn't speak English. So,

Michael stepped in. He would pretend to be the caller and ask for one of our parents, or himself. I would then reply that the person to whom he wished to speak was unavailable, and if I could take a message. We practiced that for a while until I had it down pat. In 1995, however, my parents purchased an answering machine. From that point on I didn't have to worry about the telephone.

After graduating from high school, my brother went away to college. When he moved back home with us after a while, he would crack jokes and try to make me laugh. The trouble was that I didn't "get" his jokes, so I never laughed at them. It's common for people with Asperger's not to understand jokes and subtle or dry humor. Our brains think analytically and logically, therefore many of us do not like jokes. When I told Michael that I didn't like jokes, he stopped trying to joke around with me. He understands me, and as I mentioned before, we are closer than we used to be.

One year when Halloween rolled around, there was a party for kids from kindergarten through the fifth grade. Most of the neighborhood kids I knew were going be there, which is why I didn't want to go. My parents didn't understand why I would want to miss all the fun. The truth was that I was scared to go with the other kids because I knew that two mean girls from my school would be there. I was afraid they might recognize me and start teasing me. I get enough of that at school.

Chapter Eight

Home School

FINALLY, I CAUGHT A break: home schooling!

And they say there is no God!

My mom took a job working nights so she could stay home and tutor me during the day. I was home schooled for three glorious years beginning in the sixth grade. It was the best thing that ever happened to me. At last, I was able to stay in my own comfortable world. No more teachers to deal with, no more putting up with Kris, Teri, Byron, Jared, Rob, Cameron and others! Nothing compares to the feeling of being safe; safe from abuse, ridicule, and not having to figure out what uncomfortable tones of voice meant.

You can't imagine how good it felt not to cry every day! Besides that, being home schooled was actually fun. Sometimes I had school over the weekends but that was okay. It was more than worth it! During that time, I took piano lessons, and went to operas and plays. My parents also took me to the Smithsonian Institute and all kinds of other places, as well.

The work itself was difficult. Although I tried hard to get the right answers, I *did* cheat a few times. It didn't happen often; only when I truly could not figure out the correct answer.

At the end of every school year, I was supposed to take a test at the school with all the other kids. I was afraid to go though, because I thought some of the kids might recognize me. I didn't want to go through that torment and bullying again. So, rather than my going to the school, my parents paid a licensed teacher to administer the test at our home.

Over the next two years, I had to go to school for a speech class a few times a week. The teacher was nice to me and I didn't mind it so much.

Chapter Nine

High School: Instant Replay

THE THREE YEARS OF bliss that home schooling brought passed much too quickly. Before I knew it, I was thrown back to the wolves, meaning the high school system. Unfortunately, I had to go back because I needed to accumulate credits in order to graduate.

Not much had changed during my absence. The bullies and mean kids had simply grown into bigger bullies and meaner kids.

I had not changed much, either. At school, I was still anxious, afraid, constantly worried that something was going to happen. The only good part was that I went to school half a day, so there wasn't lunch in the cafeteria to contend with. In addition, my dad took me to school and picked me up every day.

Still, they bullied me.

The first altercation was with one of my teachers, Ms. Quintana. She and I got off on the wrong foot and stayed that way. I never quite understood what it was she wanted from me. One morning she asked me if I had my book. It was unclear to which book she referred, since I had more than one I asked, "Which one?"

"Don't start that!" I am not sure, but I *think* Ms. Quintana used a certain tone of voice that scared me. The more I struggled, the more she used that tone of voice. She was mean. I tried to explain to my parents the trouble I was having with this teacher but they didn't think it was a big deal.

It was a big deal to me, though, because Ms. Quintana continuously used that tone of voice with me, even while I was stressing about the computer. She seemed to talk too fast. Either that or I wasn't listening. I mean to listen but sometimes I can't if someone is talking too fast or if they are using a certain tone of voice. Who can concentrate when they're scared?

On the days when my dad was unable to take me to school, I'd have to ride the bus, which was *always* late. Consequently, I would be late to school. The kids would make fun of me for being late to class, and say that the teacher was going to kick my butt. I believed them, of course, so that was another thing for me to worry about.

This one kid in particular gave me a lot of grief. Mitch was his name. Once he grabbed my mechanical pencil and refused to give it back to me. He would tease me and say, "Here, you can have it. . . ." and yank it away as I would reach for it. Then, he would say "Seriously, c'mon. You can have it back . . ." and yank it away. This went on and on until finally I managed to get Ms. Quintana's attention by pointing at Mitch. She was not nearly as much help as I'd hoped. In fact, she was useless. Her response to my dilemma was that I should have told Mitch not to mess with my pencil.

Yeah, right.

One time, during lunch a group of boys got together and tried to lift one another up. It's where one guy sits on a chair and four other guys try to lift him into the air with the tips of their fingers. It's spooky. Anyway, when they wanted me to try it I refused. For one thing, I didn't want to get into trouble with Ms. Quintana. For another thing, I didn't trust those boys. Why should I? I knew they would drop me. They just wanted to drop me so they could all laugh at me again.

It was just like the time in class when Mike and Billy wanted me to run around and flap my arms as if I were flying. They kept on and on, asking me to do that. They wouldn't take no for an answer. I was scared, so I did what they said. Ms. Quintana yelled at me for running around flapping my arms like a bird, but I was unable to explain that it was not my idea. I felt as if I was struggling in a raging river. The only one who could rescue me was my mom. I needed my mom to rescue me from this horrible place.

Chapter Ten

Ms. Quintana: Teacher Dearest

AGAIN, I DON'T KNOW which was worse, dealing with the students or the teachers. Ms. Quintana was just as mean and intimidating. One time right before we were about to take a final exam, she asked me if I had studied the science words from the beginning of the semester. My reply was, "No." because I hadn't studied them. She then said that she was disappointed in me for not studying the right material. How was I to know that the final exam would contain all the material we'd learned? No one told me! If they wanted me to study everything from the beginning of the year, someone should have brought it to my attention.

Another time, Ms. Quintana walked up to my desk and asked me to use the word "incline" in a sentence. I couldn't think of a way to do that, and I started getting nervous. She would not let me move until I used that word in a sentence. Finally, I said, "I don't know," because I didn't. Ms. Quintana replied that mine was not an acceptable answer. So there I sat for what seemed like hours, trying to come up with a sentence with the word "incline" in it. Ms. Quintana said, "I'm waiting . . . Are you thinking or wasting time?" The harder I tried to think the more upset I became. Apparently, my expression revealed my inner feelings because Ms. Quintana said, "Uh, uh, uh! Don't get upset!"

I was so close to bursting into tears. I experienced that drowning sensation again, as if I were trying to swim in mud. I never wanted my mother to rescue me so bad in my life! Eventually, after about ten forevers, I was able to come up with a sentence that suited Ms. Quintana.

Before I forget, let me clue you all in on a little secret. Tickling is not funny, at least not to me. It's bad enough for a person without Asperger's but for someone like me who is prone to panic attacks and doesn't like to be touched, relentless tickling is pure hell. There was this kid, a 12th-grader named Daniel, who thought it was great fun to tickle me until I laughed so hard I couldn't breathe. The other students would gather around and laugh while this was happening to me. It's just plain mean to take advantage of someone, regardless of a disability. Daniel and Conor tickled me many times, and when they found out humming the Pink Panther tune bugged me, they began to do it constantly. It drove me nuts and made me nervous.

As usual, Ms. Quintana was of no help. Her response was, "Just tell them to stop." A few times she *did* tell Daniel and Conor to leave me alone but they ignored her. Whenever I'd hear them hum the Pink Panther tune, I'd get that drowning sensation. There was no one to rescue me; not even my mom. Can *you* imagine feeling *that* helpless and afraid nearly every day of your life?

Try. I'll bet you can't!

I wish that Daniel, Conor, Mitch, Billy and all those other bullies could read my journal. Then they could know what kind of hell I endured at their hands. They probably don't even remember me now, but the torture their teasing and taunting inflicted will never go away. Wounds that are on the inside sometimes never heal. They need to know that. They also need to know how many panic attacks their bullying caused.

One day, I had finally had enough. Daniel and Conor were bothering me and something inside me snapped. I told them off big time, yelling at them to stop humming the Pink Panther tune and quit that awful tickling. I don't know if it was the right thing to do or not, but I became aggressive with my yelling.

The doctors said it was in my best interest to be around other kids. Boy, were they ever wrong! All that did was give other kids the opportunity to torture me. If only I could have been home schooled during the 1996-1997 school year! When I think about the unnecessary anxiety and torture I endured, it makes me sick.

On the brighter side of life, I did manage to have one friend. He was an African-American kid from the Bronx, named Karim.

One time we were talking and he asked me what I wanted to be when I grew up. I told him that I wanted to be a waiter. He countered with a strange question: "Wouldn't you rather be a chef?" It confused me and I had no answer for him. If I wanted to be a chef I would have said so. I wanted to be a waiter, not a chef. I didn't understand why he asked me that.

Another time I was eating my snack right before the bus came to pick me up at 11:00 am. Karim asked me why I was not eating a real lunch. The truth was that I ate my lunch at home every day because I left school at 11:00 am. I didn't tell him that, though. I don't know why, but I didn't want to tell him.

Having Karim as a friend wasn't always easy. He had a way of confusing me. The first time it happened was in May of 1997 during the week before the last week of school. Ms. Quintana had asked us to clear out the storage room. As Karim and I worked on the project he kept repeating, "C'mon, Marc! Help me! Stop wasting my time!" He used that certain tone of voice that scared me. I tried to help but he'd keep repeating, "Wait, wait. Wait a minute!" Then he would say, "Is this correct? I don't think so. I don't think so . . ."

Talk about sending mixed messages! Then Ms. Quintana came in to check on our progress. It was then that she told me to stop being lazy. Between Karim and Ms. Quintana, I was so rattled that I cried tears of pain.

I didn't understand what either of them expected of me, so how could I be lazy? None of it made sense. I began to lose confidence in Karim over that ordeal. It's hard to trust someone who confuses you. I still considered him my friend, but I never saw him again. His mother had passed away and he ended up withdrawing from school.

I wish Ms. Quintana could see what I wrote about her in my journal. That is unlikely though. If only she could know how she made me feel. Nobody should ever be made to feel that way, especially by a teacher. She and the mean students thought I was stupid because I didn't talk much. In reality, it was the other way around. Is it *smart* to bully people with disabilities? How *smart* is it for a teacher not to understand her students' with special needs? Ms. Quintana never "got" it, nor did she even try. She would have made a better drill sergeant than a teacher.

Gabriela, a girl I had a lot of trouble with, asked me why I didn't talk and if I was retarded. She was speaking to me in Spanish, by the way. Then she hit me in the arm and said, "Talk! C'mon on! Talk!" I wonder what she wanted me to say. I mean, really! She then clapped her hands in front of my face and said, "Wake up!" I wished at that time I could wake up from the nightmare of Gabriela.

My family says that I should forgive the people who made my life a living hell when I was younger. I don't think I can do it—not yet, anyway. They caused too much pain, too many times. I feel as if there are scars on my heart from them.

On the other hand, sometimes I got lucky and found people who were friendly. One girl, a twelfth-grader named Jeanette, helped me when I was having trouble with a test. I studied for it, and thought I'd remember everything when the time came, but my mind was blank. It was so nice of her to help me. There were also two boys, Travis and Lucas, who didn't give me a hard time. Both boys had speech impediments.

Chapter Eleven

Misadventures with my Classmates

IN MATH CLASS, I preferred to sit far away from the rest of the students. It made me feel more comfortable to be alone rather than crowded. This boy named Russ asked why I was sitting so far away and isolated myself. I didn't reply, so he invited his friends to come over and sit by me. Unfortunately, they did just that. Soon, there were all these boys crowded around me and Julio decided to tickle me. Matt was touching me too, but I am not sure if it was a tap or a poke, or what. I was scared and started to panic. Why did they have to bother me? A nice boy named Li told Russ and his friends to leave me alone.

Russ asked me again why I wasn't sitting closer to the other students. I finally replied that there were no empty seats for me.

"You're lying!"

How could he say that to me! That was very rude. The truth of the matter was that I was too shy to sit with the other kids. I didn't think they wanted to talk to me or hear what I had to say. Besides, they would probably talk about things that didn't interest me or say something offensive and insulting. Next, for some odd reason, Russ wanted to "high five" me. I didn't want to, but I touched his hand with my fingers. Well, that wasn't good enough for Russ—he wanted my whole hand. So, I touched his hand with my whole hand. It was the only way to get him to leave me alone.

The next time I went to class, Russ yelled as I walked in, "Empty seats! Empty seats!"

That happened the same day Ernesto asked me for the answer to a math problem on our homework assignment. I am never sure how to handle situations like this. I get very uncomfortable in social situations because I am not sure what to do. It confuses me. Finally, I went to Ms. Medina and asked her if students were supposed to give other students the answers to a problem. I said something like that, and I'm pretty sure the answer was no. I can't remember exactly what she said, but I think Ms. Medina said, "No."

Then she asked me why I had asked her that question, so I told her about Ernesto.

Later that day, Ernesto apologized to me for what he did, or tried to do. The whole situation was confusing for me, which is the norm for people with Asperger's Disorder.

We don't catch on to the innuendos, plays on words and other people's senses of humor.

Another confusing situation occurred when Ms. Medina asked me if I wanted to work on a project or something with Jimar. I said no. Maybe I should have said "no thank you." I probably meant to say that. The thing is that I prefer to work alone. Well, Jimar got a strange look on his face when I said no. I am not sure but I think he gave me that look because of the way I said "no."

That same semester Jimar asked me if I liked people of different ethnic groups. I didn't know how to handle the situation at all. It made me remember those times on the school bus when the bullies asked me all kinds of questions and I never knew which answer to give them. No matter what I answered, yes or no, they still picked on me. So, I said no, and was embarrassed at having to answer his question. All of my dealings with Jimar were confusing and made me uncomfortable.

I did not know what the difference was. I wasn't trying to be mean or hurt anyone's feelings. It's just that I don't know how to handle those kinds of situations. It was so confusing to me, but I think he was asking me those kinds of questions to get me in trouble.

I needed to be rescued by my mom and home-schooled again. I hated school. It brought me nothing but confusion and tears of pain. I was always afraid something was going to happen to me while I was there. The doctors were so wrong when they said it was best for me to be with other kids.

For instance, there was this boy named Lyle whose nickname for me was *Paranoia*. He would call me that or say, "Yo, Paranoid!" Lyle didn't understand why I was quiet all the time, so he assumed I was paranoid, I guess. Lyle gave me a hard time that semester. I had that same feeling of drowning and being unable to swim when I had to deal with Lyle, as I did with the kids I mentioned earlier. Would the bullying and teasing *never* stop?

Oh, how I wish I could have been home-schooled again!

In another direction, math was my best subject. All the other kids would try to get the answers from me—Rob, especially. I told him that I didn't know the answers, but Jenny said, "Oh, you know the answers, Marc. You just won't tell!" Irma, luckily, stood up for me and said it would be cheating if I told them the answers. That's exactly what *I* was thinking! I gathered up my books and papers and moved to another part of the room. Ms. Medina had heard what was going on and she said, "Good thinking. That's what you were supposed to do." Looking back, I am not sure if I had done the right thing or not. I was at a loss when it came to such situations. I didn't know how to handle them and I wished my mom would have been there to rescue me.

Sometimes in Ms. Hunter's second period class, we would have to break into groups, which I truly did not like. I was uncomfortable working in groups with other kids. They didn't want to be around me and that made me uncomfortable being around them. I had a hard time understanding the other kids, too. Ms. Hunter made us form two teams in order to play a game called "Taboo." It's a game in which you have one minute to describe a word written on a card, without using certain words in the description. If one of your teammates figured out the word, then your team would get one point.

We had to play this game on the Friday before Thanksgiving, prior to the school party. I ended up with Irma and Klara, but they didn't want me in their team. Klara suggested that I go over to the other group, but I didn't want to. Irma asked me also, but I refused. They kept asking and I kept telling them no. Those girls were making me nervous but finally they stopped.

I would rather have just watched the other kids play, rather than being on a team, myself. There's too much pressure from the teammates. It would be better for me if I could play solo against another solo contestant. That way there is no pressure and I would be able to concentrate. I get flustered when my teammates keep repeating, "C'mon, Marc! C'mon, Marc!" It only confuses me and makes it more difficult to describe the word. Plus, I wasn't sure if they were pressuring me, or trying to give me confidence by repeating, "C'mon, Marc!"

When it was my turn, I had to describe the word, "needle". I took the whole minute trying to describe that word but no one guessed it correctly. I had the option to pass, and move on to the next word, but I didn't do that. I stuck with needle. The worst part about playing "Taboo" was when the kids were all guessing words while I was trying to think of a way to explain it without using certain words. There was too much happening at once. I remember feeling that my teammates thought I wasn't trying hard enough.

I hated playing Taboo as much as I hated being at school.

One time Russ took a pencil, marked up his social studies book, and tried to blame it on me. When I denied marking up the book, Russ demanded that I prove it. I explained again that I was innocent, and he told me again to, "Prove it!" I erased the pencil marks he'd made in his book. That's how I proved it. End of story!

Pretty *smart*, huh?

Finally the day came when I graduated High School! I had worked so hard for this day and it was finally here! It felt so good getting my diploma.

Chapter Twelve

Making Friends 101: Waving

FOR PEOPLE WITH ASPERGER'S, it isn't easy making friends. Even those of us on the Asperger's A-List get lonely, so I try to make friends. I have good luck when I go grocery shopping. The ladies working there are friendly—they return my waves and smiles. Communicating with men is different; they are not open to being friends with me and give me strange looks, like the time the security guy followed me because I "looked suspicious." I was just doing my grocery shopping like everyone else! I avoid children completely because they might make fun of me. Lord knows I've had enough of that!

One time my brother Michael brought his girlfriend over to our house. I liked her a lot. Her name was Jacqueline. I wanted to talk to her but all I did was giggle a couple of times and look away. I was so nervous! I did manage to sit next to her on the couch, though. We sat so close that I could put my head on her shoulder. I almost did, in fact. Jackie laughed, which made me feel better.

Over the Memorial Day weekend in 1994, my parents took me to the beach. As we were lying on the beach, my mom noticed I'd been looking at a gorgeous blonde lady for quite a while. She told me to stop staring. Another time that same weekend, I was walking on the beach and waved at a lady. She waved back and said hello to me.

I had good luck at the beach, for the most part. One time, during the summer of 1999 I went to Tampa with my parents. I was sitting on the beach by myself, just goofing around and writing the names of all my favorite professional wrestlers in the sand with my finger. All of a sudden, this lady and her little girl came up to me and asked what I was doing. The lady didn't use a mean tone of voice or anything, she was just curious. She introduced herself and her daughter, Darlene and Angie were their names. Then her husband came over and we all had a pleasant conversation. They were a very nice and respectful family. It was a great experience because they didn't treat me like I was stupid. For a long time after that, whenever I went to the beach I always wrote in the sand.

Sometimes waving works out and other times it doesn't. You don't always know how it will go until it's too late. When my dad was helping me deliver papers one morning, we pulled up next to a lady who was waiting at the same stop light. I waved to her and she gave me "The Look." Another time I waved at a pregnant lady who was walking by while I was waiting in the car. She waved back at first, but then she waved her index finger at me. Apparently, I had done something improper.

Another time, in 1995, while my dad and I were waiting for my mom to get off work I waved at a lady. I guess she didn't like it because she came over to our car and talked to my dad about something. My dad wasn't happy about it so from then on I only waved to people I knew.

Nevertheless, by 2000 after I'd graduated from high school, I had become a journeyman waver. I waved at everyone in the neighborhood. There is no telling how many times I waved at people; still it brought me no friends—except for Adrienne. She was 15-years old and lived on my street. She attended the same high school as me, and was three years my junior. Sometimes she'd stop and talk to me on my front porch. Once Adrienne asked me if I knew Alonzo and Nicholas, both were special education students like me. I knew them, but not very well. Adrienne said something about Nicholas wetting his pants, or whatever.

That reminds me of another time. I was talking to Nicholas and he asked me if I liked or hated Ms. Quintana. Although she was mean to me I didn't know how to answer Nicholas' question. I wish I had told my mom about Ms. Quintana. Anyway, since I wouldn't give Nicholas a straight answer he said, "Don't tell me you *like* Ms. Quintana!" Fearing I would get in trouble, no matter what I said, I simply kept quiet.

That's the trouble with Asperger's or being autistic. You never know what people expect from you. You are always afraid of saying or doing the wrong thing. It's a constant guessing game and when you are wrong, it can cause a lot of trouble.

That didn't keep me from experimenting, though. In 2001, my cousin Daisy passed away. On the way back from her funeral, I made an evil-looking face out the car window at some girls in another car. I squished my eyebrows down and smiled the nastiest smile I could manage. The girls gave me a dirty look in return. I just wanted to see what would happen.

Chapter Thirteen

Marc vs. Vocational School

AFTER GRADUATING FROM HIGH school, I wanted to find a job and go to work. My parents wanted me to continue school so I'd have an easier way in life. I truly didn't want to go back to school, but felt obligated, so off I went to our local vocational school. Maybe it wouldn't be so bad, I kept telling myself. Maybe it would be nothing like my high school years.

I was wrong. My peers there had elevated bullying to an art form. Not all of them, of course — some simply ignored me. There was this one guy named Gregory who drove me nuts. He was always asking personal questions and bothering me. Once he tried to get me to touch a girl's buttocks. When I refused, he was very unhappy. He kept asking me, "What's wrong with you? What's your problem?" Finally, I got sick of it and told him that *he* was my problem. It turned out that's all it took to get him to leave me alone. Gregory immediately turned his attention to someone else. I don't know how long I put up with his asking me what my problem was.

I did the best I could in my merchandising courses at the vocational school and earned stock clerk certificate. There was the opportunity to further my education but I'd had enough of school, teachers, bullies, and kids like Gregory. This was no different from high school. Who needs it?

Instead, I enrolled at Vocational Rehabilitation, which eventually led to my job at a local tourist attraction.

Chapter Fourteen

My First Job

NOW, I WAS READY to face the real world as a member of America's workforce!

It was challenging at best, trying to find a job. Making the transition between school and work can be extremely difficult for Asperger's people. In addition, once employers learn you have autism, you are **done**. The job coach assigned to me by Vocational Rehabilitation put his heart and soul into helping me with my job search. I lost track of how many employers we tried, all with the same results. The trick was to find an employer willing to give me a chance, one who would accept and work with my limitations rather than against them. Eventually, our perseverance paid off and I landed a job at one of the local tourist attractions.

There, I became an Operations Host. It was not was not a good fit for me but, what choice did I have? Dealing with tourists and being in charge of crowd control was definitely not my specialty. A special needs person such as me had no business being in charge of crowd control, answering questions for tourists, and trying to get people to follow directions. Many times I'd answer questions with an "I don't know."

One time a man tried to get me to let him and his adult daughter into one of the areas before it was even open. The man said they had an early appointment. It was against the rules to let visitors in until 10:00, so I told them to check with the information center, and he said he'd done that and was told to come to my area and I would let them in.

Still, I refused. It was against the rules and I always follow the rules.

That's when the trouble really started. He asked to speak to my manager. Well, I became so nervous and confused that I couldn't even look at the man and his daughter, let alone reply to them. I just stood there staring at the ground. There must have been a tragic look on my face because a crowd had gathered and people were telling me to calm down. Even the man and his daughter were being nice and telling me not to be upset. They seemed to feel guilty for upsetting me.

One lady came up to me and asked if I was diabetic. No, I am not diabetic. I have Asperger's Disorder.

Another incident occurred on August 28, 2002. I was working the 8:30 am to 4:00 pm shift and had a problem with a man from Europe. I asked him to get off the grass at dockside and he asked me why. My response was that he was too close to the water and might fall in.

"Up yours!" "Forget you!" "The heck with you!" the man from Europe yelled at me, refusing to get off the grass. I'm putting it delicately because I am a gentleman. He had used vulgar language. At first, I thought he was goofing around, but he was serious. As I mentioned before, one thing about Asperger's is that it's difficult to gauge other people's mindset and what their intentions are.

Oh and then there was a lady pushing a disabled baby in a stroller. I didn't know the baby was disabled until she told me. Anyway, she claimed to be with some organization and that an associate said she could go inside with her baby. I then gave my usual hand/arm signal for her and the baby to enter. Rather than proceeding, she asked to speak to the manager. This confused me. I mean, I was allowing her to go inside but she wanted to talk to my manager. She used a harsh of voice with me for no reason. It didn't make any sense to me, and I just stared at her. Then she asked me if I always wave at disabled babies.

What she was talking about, I will never know. I was completely lost. Then she started screaming at me in a shrill ugly voice, "Because that is so rude!"

I was speechless as I attempted to puzzle it out in my mind: "Why is she asking me this question?" "What gave her the impression that I am rude? I didn't do anything wrong." Besides, I am a disabled person myself, so there is no way I'd ever be rude to another disabled person, especially a baby. She was the rude one, not me.

As you can see, that job was terribly stressful for me. Every work day I left with a headache and had to take painkillers nearly every night. After three years I'd had enough and gave my two-week notice. I *still* cannot believe that I did this for three years. I was proud leaving the company on good terms though, and so grateful to them for giving me a chance.

Chapter Fifteen

About Me and My Life

I AM STILL SHY but have come a long way. I am happy working as a volunteer, going out to dinner and outings with my family and friends, listening to music, keeping track of music charts —I can name almost every artist and their music. I love dancing, and of course, there is my writing. I like it when family comes over, especially when my brother Michael stops by. He and I discuss boxing, sports and TV shows. My favorite is this reality show where teams have cooking competitions, although sometimes I get upset with all the yelling. It reminds me of what I went through in school and makes me feel distressed and angry. It is almost as if I am reliving the bullying and teasing when the characters on the show are being yelled at or belittled. I know it's just part of the show, but I feel like writing to the show's writers and asking them to make the characters friendlier. I find it very upsetting and frustrating when people are mean to others.

It's great when Michael takes me to the beach for the whole weekend, just us guys. Michael also keeps me up to date on the latest in technology. I'm a fast learner with a phenomenal memory.

I used to love going to the arcades when I was younger. I loved them because they provided an escape to the boredom and loneliness I used to feel. I outgrew my need for that, though. In addition to the reality show, I love the old TV shows like *I Dream of Jeannie* and *Bewitched* reruns. My brother bought me the entire collection of every episode of all the season's shows for Christmas one year. My brother Michael is the best!

As far as friends, I belong to a meet-up group for adults with Asperger's Syndrome. I like to go on their trips, as long as they are not too far away. Sometimes I go out to dinner with friends. I also belong to the local chapter of the Autism Society, which offers enjoyable events and outings for members and families. Lately I've been mingling with the people in my mom's groups. I've met some nice ladies there who are friendly and like me a lot. My mom and I attend many community events and do volunteer work together. Sometimes my dad goes to the events as well. It's a good thing for me because I have the opportunity to spend time with "regular" people away from my groups, like the other day when I was volunteering at the YMCA and played basketball with someone there for a long time. I like the social media to stay in touch with family and some of my co-workers from my old jobs.

I love to travel with my parents and go on cruises. Every year we go on vacation and I always get to pick the place.

In addition, I am thinking about taking up piano lessons again someday. I can already read music, and with practice, I could probably become pretty good someday.

I really want to get my own place, too. It's time for me to be independent. I know my life skills to perfection. Although I do not drive, I am able to get around town quite well.

In the meantime, I will continue to write my stories. My specialty is sad fiction. Although this book is sad in parts, it is *not* fiction. What you've read here is 100% true experience.

It is the story of my life.

Anyway, my mom says that the characters I create in my stories remind her of me. I write them in hopes of recovering from the taunting and bullying that plagued me throughout my life.

I hope my book has helped you and others who've read it to understand Asperger's Disorder and autism, and what it's like for a people on the Asperger's A-List. I also hope that the next time you meet someone like me, you will be kind to them. Now that you know a little about Asperger's Disorder and autism, put yourself in our place and imagine how you would feel. Kindness matters. If you do this, the world will be a better place for all concerned.

It is my wish to have the opportunity to meet other individuals who, like me, have cried tears of pain while struggling and longing for acceptance in your world — a world that is so different from ours.

I want to tell them that I no longer cry tears of pain.

NOTE OF CHANGE FROM ASPERGER'S TO AUTISM

As of May 2013, Asperger's will be made part of a single diagnosis: Autism spectrum disorder.

American Psychiatric Association Board of Trustees Approves DSM-5

December 1, 2012

by the American Psychiatric Association

The criteria will incorporate several diagnoses from DSM-IV including Asperger's Disorder into the diagnosis of autism spectrum disorder for DSM-5 to help more accurately and consistently diagnose children with autism.

www.ingramcontent.com/pod-product-compliance
Lightning Source LLC
Chambersburg PA
CBHW071409160426
42813CB00092B/3444/J